GUINNESS W★RLD RECORDS

UP CLOSE

Wild Weather

Compiled by Kris Hirschmann and Ryan Herndon

For Guinness World Records: Laura Barrett Plunkett, Craig Glenday, Stuart Claxton, Michael Whitty, and Laura Jackson

SCHOLASTIC INC.

New York Toronto London Auckland Sydney
Mexico City New Delhi Hong Kong Buenos Aires

© 2007 Guinness World Records Limited, a HIT Entertainment Limited Company.

ISBN-13: 978-0-439-89828-7
ISBN-10: 0-439-89828-5

Designed by Michelle Martinez Design, Inc.
Photo Research by Els Rijper, Alan Gottlieb
Records from the Archives of Guinness World Records

12 11 10 9 8 7 6 5 4   9 10 11/0

Printed in the U.S.A.

First printing, January 2007

Visit Guinness World Records at www.guinnessworldrecords.com

ZOOM IN!

For more than 50 years, Guinness World Records has
documented the most amazing record-breakers around the globe.
Today, the records in their archives number more than 40,000.

In this collection, we'll zoom in on 25 wild weather-related
records. We'll get swept up in the awesome power of tornadoes,
hurricanes, and other windy events. We'll sweat it out in some hot
spots, and we'll get the chills shivering through some incredibly
cold conditions. Finally, we'll take a peek at the "Best of the Best"
— five entries so extreme, they simply blow away the competition.

Go up close and get electric — Guinness World Records style!

A Record-Breaking History

The idea for Guinness World Records grew out [of] question. In 1951, Sir Hugh Beaver, the managing direc[tor] of the Guinness Brewery, wanted to know which was [the] fastest game bird in Europe — the golden plover or [the] grouse? Some people argued that it was the grouse. Oth[ers] claimed it was the plover. A book to settle the debate [did] not exist until Sir Hugh discovered the knowledgeable tw[in] brothers Norris and Ross McWhirter, who lived in Londo[n.]

Like their father and grandfather, the McWhirter tw[ins] loved information. They were kids just like you when they started clipping interest[ing] facts from newspapers and memorizing important dates in world history. As well [as] learning the names of every river, mountain range, and nation's capital, they knew [the] record for pole squatting (196 days in 1954), which language had only one irregular v[erb] (Turkish), and that the grouse — flying at a timed speed of 43.5 miles per hour — is fas[ter] than the golden plover at 40.4 miles per hour.

Norris and Ross served in the Royal Navy during World War II, graduated from colle[ge,] and launched their own fact-finding business called McWhirter Twins, Ltd. They w[ere] the perfect people to compile the book of records that Sir Hugh Beaver searched [for] yet could not find.

The first edition of *The Guinness Book of Records* was published on August 27, 19[55,] and since then has been published in 37 languages and more than 100 countries. In 20[00,] the book title changed to *Guinness World Records* and has set an incredible record of [its] own: Excluding non-copyrighted books such as the Bible and the Koran, *Guinness Wo[rld] Records* is the best-selling book of all time!

Today, the official Keeper of the Records keeps a careful eye on each Guinness Wo[rld] Record, compiling and verifying the greatest the world has to offer — from the fast[est] and the tallest to the slowest and the smallest, with everything in between.

Out of the Sky

"**L**ook out below!" Ridiculous rainfall, lengthy lightning, humungous hailstones, and super-size snowflakes are coming your way. So open your umbrella . . . and duck your head. When wild weather looms, you never know what may fall out of the sky!

When is a fossil *not* a fossil?

When it's a pseudofossil, of course! The word *pseudofossil* means "false fossil," and it refers to ancient markings that were not created by living organisms. Preserved dinosaur bones, plant leaves, worm holes, and mammoth footprints are all fossils. Old mineral growths, gas bubbles in rocks, and — you guessed it — craters from a long-ago rainfall are *not* fossils, according to scientists. But hey, it's just a term, and a fossil by any other name looks just as old.

Oldest Fossilized Raindrops

If you're planning to hop into your time machine and the ancient past, remember to take an umbrella along. Ye rained back then, too. Indian geologist Chirananda De prove on December 15, 2001, when he announced his discovery of **Oldest Fossilized Raindrops** in the lower Vindhyan moun range in Madhya Pradesh, India. The prehistoric precipita occurred about 1.6 billion years ago, leaving impact craters damp layer of sediment. When the sediment hardened into r the ⅛-inch-wide indentations became a permanent record some old wet weather. The primeval pockmarks might not so like a big deal, but to geologists, these findings are exciting. " finding could help in establishing the atmospheric condition Earth millions of years ago," exclaimed one scientist. Pictu below is an extreme close-up of some fossilized raindrops f the Northeastern USA region.

UP CLOSE

FACT:

It probably didn't rain much 1.6 billion years ago. If it did, Chirananda De's rain craters would have been washed away long before they could harden.

The difference between drizzle and rain

DRIZZLE: Drops with diameter smaller than .02 inch falling close together.

RAIN: Drops with diameter larger than .02 inch, or smaller drops widely separated.

A TOTAL WASHOUT

Rainfall is often described as light, moderate, or heavy. Light rainfall is anything less than 0.1 inch per hour. Moderate rainfall is anywhere between 0.1 and 0.3 inch per hour, and heavy rainfall is anything over 0.3 inch. How bad is a heavy rainfall? You would be rapidly soaked if caught outside in a heavy rainfall without an umbrella. Imagine that experience and then multiply the downpour by 300 times — that was Basse-Terre's record-soaking storm!

During a hard rain, people sometimes say it's "raining cats and dogs." But most cats and dogs are too smart to go outside in this type of wild weather!

RECORD 2
Most Intense Rainfall

When you think about the Caribbean, you may picture [san]dy beaches and sparkling water. Most people don't realize [th]at this region is the home of some mighty wild weather, too! [Ca]se in point: On November 26, 1970, the region of Basse-[Ter]re, Guadeloupe, received a deluge of 1.5 inches of rainfall [in] a single *minute* — the **Most Intense Rainfall** ever recorded [by] modern methods. That's about the same amount of rain the [fa]mously wet city of Seattle, Washington, typically receives during [th]e entire *month* of June. The record-breaking downpour was [ex]treme even for tropical Basse-Terre, which logs up to 100 [in]ches of precipitation per year.

UP CLOSE

Of all common trees, the oak is struck most often by lightning.

Fulgurite

Dare to hold a lightning bolt in your hand.

Lightning is hot enough to melt sand upon impact. As the liquefied sand cools, it forms a glassy shape called a fulgurite that traces the path of the lightning bolt. The Longest Fulgurite ever found was dug up in 1996 in Florida. Two hollow branches — one 17 feet long and the other 16 feet long — ran down from the lightning-strike point. Professionals found this object, but anyone searching can unearth a fulgurite. "Go to any beach and start digging," explains Martin Uman, the scientist who discovered the record-shattering bolt.

RECORD 3
Longest Lightning Flash

Scientists estimate that lightning strikes somewhere arou the world 100 times every second. That's 6,000 strikes p minute . . . 360,000 strikes per hour . . . and 8.64 milli strikes per day! Most of these millions of bolts are about 5 miles long. But one lightning bolt spotted in 1956 really we the extra mile. Observed using radar and recorded by meteorologist Myron Ligda, the **Longest Lightning Fla** covered a horizontal distance of 93 miles inside clouds. It wou take a person about 90 minutes to drive that distance in a c But Myron's blazing bolt completed the journey in a **flash**!

mal hail forms inside storm clouds. Water droplets eze onto smaller objects such as dust particles, ice stals, or bugs. When the icy pellet is too heavy to stay he cloud, it falls to the ground as a hailstone.

IT'S A BIRD . . . IT'S A PLANE . . . IT'S A GIANT ICE CUBE?!?

Enormous blocks of ice have been plummeting from the sky for centuries. Scientists call these chilly chunks megacryometeors, and they have no idea where they come from or how they form. Different people have suggested that megacryometeors might be gigantic hailstones, ice chunks scraped loose from airplane wings, or unusually small comets. But none of these explanations fits. For now, megacryometeors are still a mystery — and people are still in danger of getting bonked on the head by falling pieces of sky, just like Chicken Little.

ECORD 4

argest Piece of Fallen Ice

"The sky is falling!" At first, no one believed the fictional acter of Chicken Little when he squawked these now-famous ds. But Chicken Little's buddies might have paid closer attention heir panicky pal if they had been in Ross-shire, Scotland, UK, August 13, 1849. On that day, a 20-foot-long chunk of ice mmeted from the evening sky and crashed onto the ground of cal farm. Estimated to weigh about 1,000 pounds, the **Largest ce of Fallen Ice** was crystal-clear yet seemed to be made of y smaller shards. Scientists theorized that the chunks may have n fused together by high-altitude lightning. No matter how it formed, one thing's for sure: You don't want to play chicken a piece of ice this big.

There's science in every snowball.

Have you ever wondered what really happens when you make a snowball? Here's the scientific scoop! First, you squeeze a double fistful of loose snow into a ball. The pressure you exert makes the snow melt just a little bit. Melted snow is water, of course, and this water seeps into the tiny spaces between the still-frozen parts. When you stop squeezing, the water turns back into ice, gluing the snow particles into a ball. The wetter the snow, the thicker and heavier your snowball will be.

RECORD 5

Largest Snowflake

Does this story sound a little flaky to you? On Janua[r] 28, 1887, a snowstorm dumped gigantic flakes over t[he] state of Montana at Fort Keogh, which is near the moder[n] day town of Miles City. During the storm, rancher Ma[tt] Coleman reportedly measured a flake that was 15 inch[es] wide and 8 inches thick — the **Largest Snowflake** [on] record. This flake and the others dropped by the stor[m] were "larger than milk pans," Matt later said in a magazi[ne] interview. An unidentified mail carrier caught in the sa[me] storm agreed that the flakes were, indeed, record-worth[y.]

UP CLOSE

Six Different Kinds of Snow Crystals

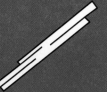
Needle Clusters

Sheaths

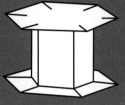
Capped Columns

Hexagonal Plates

Stellar Plates

Stellar Dendrites

Temperature and humidity change the shape of a snow crystal.

A REAL SNOW JOB

The folks who run the Mount Shasta Ski Bowl in northern California would probably laugh at the extra-big snowflakes that fell on Fort Keogh. After all, they survived the **Greatest Snowfall for a Snowstorm.** Mount Shasta's big blizzard took place between February 13 and 19, 1959, and it dumped 189 inches (that's 15.75 feet) of snow onto the mountain's upper levels. Imagine trying to shovel your driveway after *that* snowstorm!

FACT:

Smaller snow crystals stick together on their way to the ground and form a snowflake or aggregation. Flakes can grow in size from 3 to 10 inches in diameter.

Blown Away

Head for the storm shelter, because you're about to be buffete five of the breeziest entries blowing through the Guinness World Recor archives. Visit the world's windiest place, try to get up close and person with some terrible twisters, immerse yourself in a giant waterspout, and more. These records are fast, furious, and may make your head spin!

Tornado Country

There's no doubt that Mount Washington gets some wicked wind gusts. In terms of tornadoes, however, it turns out that the United Kingdom is the windiest place on the planet. This island nation reports an average of one twister per 2,856 square miles each year. That's the Most Tornadoes by Area of any country in the world. Just in case you were wondering, the equivalent figure for the United States is one tornado per 3,345 square miles.

UP CLOSE

RECORD 6
Windiest Place

How would you like to live in the center of a major hurricane, the time? Just to make the offer extra tempting, let's throw a subzero wind-chill factor to boot. These conditions don't nd appealing — but they are a way of life at the Mount shington Observatory, perched atop 6,288-foot-tall unt Washington in New Hampshire's White Mountains. this way-high way station, ferocious winds and freezing mperatures are the norm year-round. Conditions were ticularly bad on April 12, 1934, when a ground wind ed of 231 miles per hour was recorded at the **Windiest ce** on the planet. This gargantuan gust not only onished observers, it also earned Mount Washington econd Guinness World Record for having the **Fastest face Wind Speed**.

FACT:

Every June, about 1,100 runners participate in the Mount Washington Road Race. During the 7.6-mile race from the mountain's base to its summit, runners cope with snow, fog, wind, and other challenging weather conditions.

FACT:

In a large waterspout, water can swirl at speeds up to 190 miles per hour. A spout of this strength can be about 90 feet wide.

UP CLOSE

Frogs can fly when waterspouts spin nearby.

Do you believe those crazy tales of frogs, fish, and other creatures falling out of a clear blue sky? You should, because most of these stories are true! Waterspouts suck lake and sea creatures from their aquatic homes and carry them high into the air. The accidental aviators sometimes travel long distances before falling back to the ground. Here are a few recent examples of "ballistic beasties":

FISHY RAINFALLS

- Paravur, India, May 2006
- Wales, UK, August 2004

FROG AND TOAD SPRINKLES

- Serbia, July 2005
- London, England, UK, 1998

RECORD 7
Highest Waterspout

If you want to scare a sailor, shout "Waterspout!" These typ[e] of weather phenomenon are tornadoes traveling across seas [or] lakes instead of land, and capable of destroying a ship in t[he] blink of an eye. The twisting tubes of water usually form und[er] low-lying clouds, but not always. On May 16, 1898, mini[ng] engineer D. R. Crichton grabbed a theodolite, an instrume[nt] used in mountain-surveying, to measure the second watersp[out] spawned among a group of 20 swirling off the coast of Ede[n,] New South Wales, Australia. The stupendous spout was 10[ ] feet in diameter, 250 feet long, and a record-setting 5,014 fe[et] tall — the **Highest Waterspout** ever recorded.

Most Tornadoes in 24 Hours

"I was too busy to be afraid. It was just warning after warning after warning," recalls a TV meteorologist broadcasting during the tornado "Super Outbreak" of April 3-4, 1974. During this freak weather event, 148 tornadoes swept through 13 southern and midwestern states (Alabama, Georgia, Illinois, Indiana, Kentucky, Michigan, Mississippi, North and South Carolina, Ohio, Tennessee, Virginia, and West Virginia). This event marked the Most Tornadoes in 24 Hours ever recorded. The wild winds cut a devastating swath through the communities. About 5,485 people were injured, and 330 people lost their lives. Luckily, the weather conditions that created this monster storm were rare, so area residents probably will never repeat their terrifying ordeal.

CREATING A MONSTER

The tornado outbreak of April 3-4, 1974, got its start when a layer of dry air began to sink onto a layer of moist air. Moist air tends to rise, but this particular air mass couldn't because of the sinking air layer above it. As the day wore on, however, sunlight heated the moist air and energized its molecules. Eventually, the air mass grew strong enough to punch holes in the drier layer above it. Air started to blast upward through these holes, spinning and spawning tornadoes as it went.

Six tornadoes received F5 ratings in the 1974 Super Outbreak.

UP CLOSE

15

One day in May was a *really* windy day in Oklahoma.

A storm on May 3, 1999, not only spawned the widest tornado ever, it also produced a tornado that broke the Guinness World Record for the **Fastest Wind Speed**. Winds inside the ferocious funnel topped out at an incredible 302 +/- 20 mph. The sturdy "Doppler on Wheels" unit performed the measurements, which were taken near the Oklahoma town of Bridge Creek. The record-breaking reading was taken between 100 and 200 feet above the ground, so no one knows how fast the twister's winds were moving at ground level.

RECORD 9

Largest Measured Tornado

"Oklahoma is OK," says the state's auto license plate. Oklahoma definitely was *not* OK on the night of May 3, 19 when a total of 59 tornadoes spun their way across the st. One of these twisters measured an unbelievable 5,250 feet fr side to side — that's almost a mile! With its gigantic girth, tornado easily earned the Guinness World Record for **Larg Measured Tornado**. The fantastic funnel was measured University of Oklahoma professor Joshua Wurman using "Doppler on Wheels" mobile weather observatory, a rapid-s radar unit that draws a complete picture of a storm every 5 10 seconds. *Say cheese!* Now run for shelter!

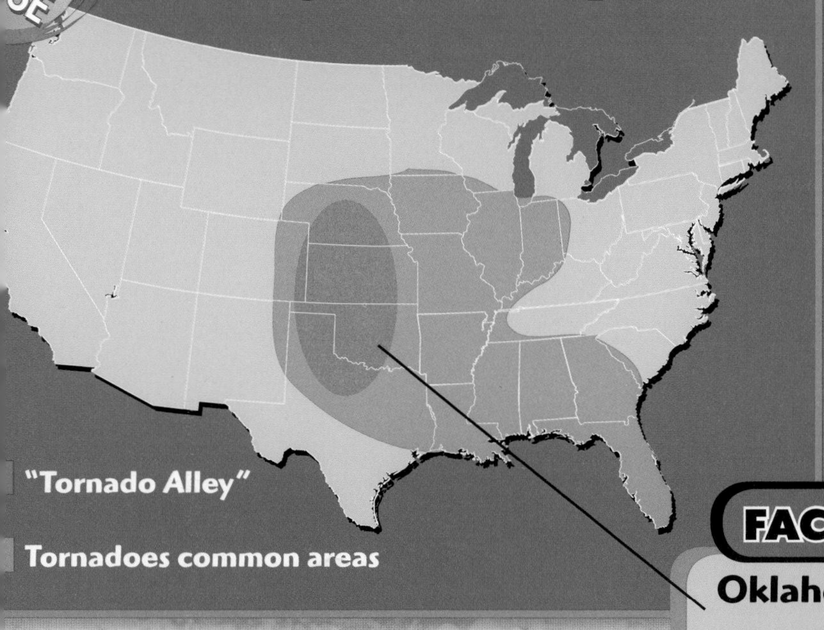

WIPED OFF THE MAP

On the morning of May 3, 1999, the sleepy little town of Mulhall, Oklahoma, had 200 residents and 113 buildings. By the end of the day, the town was literally wiped off the map. The terrible twister measured by Joshua Wurman traveled across Mulhall in the evening hours, shredding things as it went. It destroyed the elementary school and the grocery store, and severely damaged three churches and a bank. It even blew down the town's 75-foot high, 400,000-gallon water tank. This event caused a flash flood that pushed a nearby house 20 feet off its foundation. The power of wind is truly an amazing force of nature.

The area from central Texas to Nebraska is known as "Tornado Alley."

UP CLOSE

Tracking Tornado Alley

"Tornado Alley"

Tornadoes common areas

FACT: Oklahoma suffers more severe tornadoes than any other US state.

The storms on Neptune will blow you away!

The planet Neptune hosts some of the solar system's biggest cyclones. The planet's largest and most intense storm was called the Great Dark Spot, and it was discovered in 1989 by NASA's *Voyager 2* spacecraft. The system had disappeared by 1994, but it was soon replaced by a similar storm on another part of the planet. Other notable Neptunian weather systems include Scooter, which is a white cloud south of the Great Dark Spot, and the Wizard's Eye, which is a large southern hurricane.

RECORD 10

Fastest Winds in the Solar System

Conditions are breezy year-round on the planet Nep which boasts the **Fastest Winds in the Solar System**. Mea by NASA's *Voyager 2* probe in 1989, Neptune's mighty air str blast around the planet at speeds up to 1,500 miles per hour — eight times the speed of the fastest cyclones on Earth! Scie aren't sure exactly why Neptune's conditions are so extreme they suspect that the planet's fast rotation has something t with it. Even though Neptune is huge (it's about four times than Earth), it makes one complete spin approximately eve hours. All that motion probably churns up the atmosphere creates the gas giant's record-making breezes.

UP CLOS

FACT:

Neptune was discovered by math! In 1846, scientists crunched some numbers and decided that an unknown planet was making Uranus wobble in its orbit. When they pointed their telescopes at the sky, there was Neptune, exactly as pinpointed.

In Roman mythology, Neptune was the god of the sea.

EYE IN THE SKY

The US National Aeronautics and Space Administration (NASA) is thinking about sending a spacecraft to Neptune. The proposed *Neptune Orbiter* would be launched sometime around 2016 and its journey would last 8 to 12 years. Its mission would be to study Neptune's atmosphere and weather, its ring system (yes, it has one), and its moons. Scientists believe this information, gathered by satellite, would answer many questions about the "other" big blue planet.

It takes the planet Neptune almost 165 Earth years to orbit the sun.

FACT:

Neptune completes its orbit around the sun at 3.4 miles per second — equal to 12,240 miles per hour!

There's a whole universe of wild weather out there, including these bright, shining examples of extraterrestrial activity. Warm up on Venus and get toasty in the sun's fiery core, then cool off in the chilliest and windiest places ever discovered. Finally, zip back to Earth in time to experience the worst space storm. Are you ready? It's 3 . . . 2 . . . 1 . . . BLAST OFF into outer space . . . and beyond!

The Boomerang Nebula is sometimes called the Bowtie Nebula because of its shape.

Cosmic Recycling

The Boomerang Nebula is gradually becoming a Planetary nebula, a phrase that describes a glowing cloud of gas and dust surrounding a smaller, hot white star. Planetary nebulae aren't planets, but sometimes they look like planets when viewed from a distance using a telescope. It's how these clouds got their spherical names. These special clouds act as a galactic recycling center by dumping a dead star's waste gases — carbon, nitrogen, oxygen, calcium, and other minerals — back into deep space. The released minerals will eventually help to form new stars and planets.

RECORD 11

Coldest Place in the Milky Way Galaxy

According to scientists, the lowest possible temperature is -467 degrees Fahrenheit (also known as 0 degrees Kelvin). At this temperature, frozen atoms stop moving. The **Coldest Place in the Milky Way Galaxy** doesn't quite hit this bone-numbing mark, but it comes shockingly close. Located about 5,000 light-years away from Earth in the Centaurus constellation, the Boomerang Nebula has an average temperature of - 457.6 degrees Fahrenheit. Why is this nebula so chilly? The cosmic cloud of expanding gases sheds heat and makes the nebula even colder than its neighboring areas.

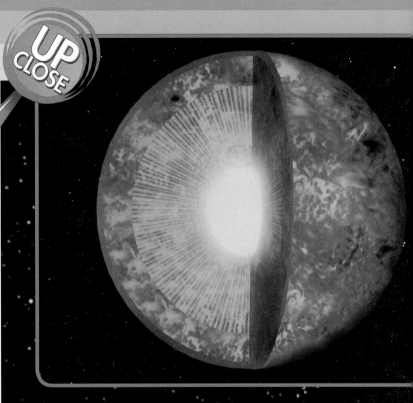

UP CLOSE

The solar system's lightbulb will be working for approximately another 5 billion years.

Scientists expect the sun to redden and swell as it enters the end phase of its life. It may even get big enough to engulf Earth. The "red giant" phase will last a few million years. After this period, the sun will eject its outer layers and shrink down into a small star called a white dwarf. It will still be extremely hot, but it will not be big enough to heat up the solar system the way it does today.

FACT:

The temperature of the sun's visible surface is just over 10,000 degrees Fahrenheit.

RECORD 12

Hottest Place in the Solar System

Earth's equator? Hot. The Sahara Desert? HOT. A volca lava bath? EEEEYOW!!! But these scorching places are cold compared to the sun's core, which is by far the **Hott Place in the Solar System**. Humans have not yet inven a safe way to visit the center of the sun, but scientists beli that temperatures in this hot spot reach about 28,080,0 degrees Fahrenheit! Intense pressure — about 250 bil times the pressure at sea level on Earth — is the rea for the roasting conditions. This powerful pressure fo hydrogen atoms to combine in a process called **nucl fusion**. In turn, fusion creates the energy that heats the sun, making it the solar system's hottest object its brightest one, too.

WEATHER MAKER

Energy from the sun creates Earth's weather. It all starts when heat, light, and radiation from the sun strike our planet and heat up the atmosphere. Not much would happen if every place got the same amount of sunlight, but that's not the case. Some areas get hotter than others. As a result, the heated air molecules start bouncing around, trying to balance out its energy. Thunderstorms, hurricanes, tornadoes, and other weather events are the result.

Earth	Jupiter	Venus
Mars	Neptune	Saturn
Mercury	Sun	Uranus

Every second, the sun's superheated core converts more than 661 million tons of matter into energy.

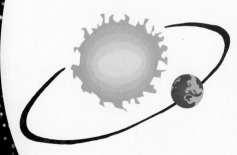

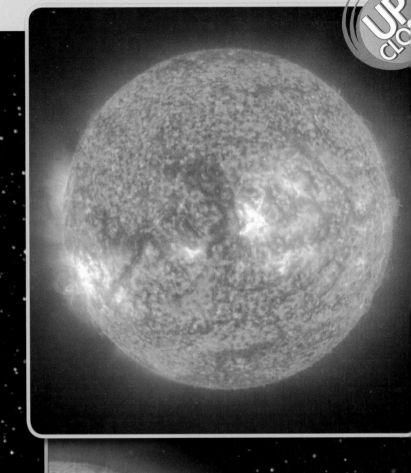

Solar wind isn't like Earth wind.

Solar wind is actually a stream of electrically charged gas racing outward from the sun at speeds up to 550 miles per second. Under normal conditions, the solar wind blows fairly steadily. But sometimes the sun "burps" and releases an extra-large gas bubble in an event called a coronal mass ejection (CME). CMEs often occur along with solar flares, which are spectacular fiery eruptions on the sun's surface. These eruptions can't be seen with the naked eye, but special telescopes have allowed scientists to photograph them in fabulous, flaming detail.

FACT:

You can't see or feel a geomagnetic storm — but if you were in space, it could kill you. An astronaut exposed to a geomagnetic storm could die of radiation poisoning within minutes. People on Earth are much safer, since our atmosphere protects us from the worst of the rays.

Most Destructive Geomagnetic Storm

Killer storms from space! They sound like science fiction but are a havoc-creating reality. Geomagnetic storms occur when particles from the sun alter Earth's magnetic field, the **magnetosphere**. The **Most Destructive Geomagnetic Storm** struck on March 13, 1989. Caused by an eruption at a large sunspot — 54 times as big as Earth — that propelled *billions of tons* of solar particles into space, the geomagnetic storm knocked out the power grid in parts of the United States and Canada, leaving about 6 million people without electricity for 9 hours! The storm also changed the orbits of satellites, caused navigation systems around the globe to go haywire, and disrupted radio and TV signals. It was classified as a 6.5 — the most severe category of storm.

FACT:

Even homing pigeons become lost during geomagnetic storms.

NATURAL FIREWORKS

The sun is responsible for an awe-inspiring natural phenomenon called the aurora borealis and australis, also known as the northern and southern lights. These multicolored displays occur when the solar wind bumps into the atmosphere near Earth's magnetic poles. When conditions are right, many forces work together to "excite" the atoms. The particles start to glow as a result and may sometimes light up the night sky. Aurora displays are usually red or greenish blue, but they can be any color of the rainbow. They are seldom seen outside the extreme northern and southern parts of Earth.

It's just a little bit backwards.

In a planet's southern hemisphere, regular cyclones spin in a clockwise direction. That's not the case on Jupiter, the largest planet in our solar system. Jupiter's Great Red Spot is an anticyclone spinning counterclockwise at a speed of 270 miles per hour. Anticyclones sometimes occur on Earth, and when they do, they usually bring calm weather. But on Jupiter, the Great Red Spot's wind speeds often reach a howling 250 miles per hour!

Jupiter is the largest planet in our solar system.

RECORD 14
Largest Cyclone in the Solar System

On Earth, people in a hurricane's path have to hun down for a few hours while the storm passes. On the pla Jupiter, they would have to hide out for at least 340 yea That's how long the **Largest Cyclone in the Solar Syste** has been raging. Known in astronomy circles as the Great R Spot, this massive storm measures up to 8,700 miles wide a 24,860 miles long — large enough to contain three Ear This super cyclone is so big that it takes about 6 Earth d to make one full turn. It keeps on spinning because Jupite made mostly of gas, which means there are no solid surfa to suck up the system's energy.

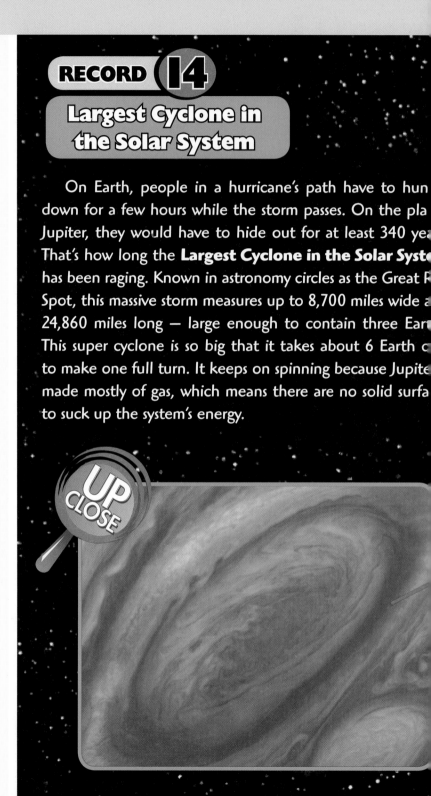

UP CLOSE

The Great Red Spot changes color. Brick red, pale salmon, and white have been the colors in recent years.

SPOT, JR.

In the year 2000, three small white storms on Jupiter joined to form one big white storm. Officially called Oval BA, the storm stayed white until February 2006, when it turned the same shade as the planet's Great Red Spot. Scientists think this change might be a sign that Oval BA is getting stronger, but no one knows for sure. Only time will tell if the Earth-size storm can become as "great" as its famous forerunner.

FACT:

In 2004, the Great Red Spot was 50 percent smaller than 100 years earlier. We don't yet know whether the storm is disappearing or it naturally swells and shrinks through the ages.

FACT:

Any smaller storms bumped into by the Great Red Spot are absorbed.

There's a reason Venus is *the* hot spot in the galaxy.

Carbon dioxide clouds blanket Venus and cause its blistering climate. Radiation from the sun easily passes through these clouds — then is trapped after turning into heat energy upon the planet's surface. Hot air molecules bounce around in Venus's atmosphere, raising temperatures. Too bad about those clouds. Without the cloud cover, scientists say, the temperatures on Venus would be similar to temperatures on Earth and we might consider inhabiting this planet!

The planet Venus is called the evening star or the morning star because it appears brightest in Earth's night sky right after sunset or before sunrise.

RECORD 15
Hottest Planet

Have you heard the expression "hot enough to fry an egg the sidewalk"? You could make scrambled eggs on the pathw of planet Venus if it *had* sidewalks, and if the eggs surviv the landing during your space journey. Venus checks in as **Hottest Planet** in the solar system. Daytime temperatu on Earth's closest neighbor can soar to a blazing 896 degr Fahrenheit — that's hot enough to melt lead! Unfortunately scientists, it is also hot enough to ruin any man-made equipme that enters the planet's fiery atmosphere. For this reason, m of the planet's exploration has been conducted in outer spa Orbiting craft use radar and other no-touch methods to coll information about the sizzling sphere.

Weathered Sites

Pack your sunglasses and an insulated winter coat before touring these places famous for consistently way-out weather conditions. From the hottest hamlet to the iciest outpost, from the driest desert to the soggiest city, these record-holders prove that wild weather isn't always a one-time event. Sometimes, it's a way of everyday life.

What you see isn't always what you get.

When it comes to temperature readings, the thermometer doesn't tell the full story. Moisture in the air, called humidity, can make the air feel hotter than the numbers suggest. How much of an effect does humidity have? On July 8, 2003, the official temperature in Dhahran, Saudi Arabia, was 108 degrees Fahrenheit. However, the high humidity made it feel like 176 degrees in the shade, and a sweltering 191 degrees in the sun! Sounds like a good day to sit inside an air-conditioned room and read the newest edition of *Guinness World Records*.

Atlantic Ocean

Al'Aziziyah

TUNISIA

Mediterranean Sea

MOROCCO

WESTERN SAHARA

ALGERIA

LIBYA

EGYPT

MAURITANIA

MALI

SAHARA DESERT

AFRICA

ETHIOP

FACT:

A place called Dakol in Ethiopia's Danakil Depression average a blistering 94 degrees Fahrenheit — Earth's highest mean temperature. Amazingly, some people call this place home. T make a living, they sell slabs of salt pried from the parched pl

RECORD 16

Highest Recorded Temperature

Think the **Highest Recorded Temperature** occurs in t superheated heart of a desert? Think again! On Septemb 13, 1922, the thermometer topped out at an incredible degrees Fahrenheit in the Libyan town of Al'Aziziyah, wh is located just a few miles south of the Mediterranean S Admittedly, Al'Aziziyah does fall within the northernmost ed of the Sahara Desert, but that area is not usually the hott part of the desert. For this reason, scientists think that oth unmeasured areas may have been even hotter than Al'Aziziy on that blazing September day. "It is not out of the questi that somewhere else in northwestern Libya, the temperatu exceeded 136 degrees," explains one scientist. Now *that'* scorcher of a day!

Vostok Station 11,220 feet above sea level.

TOUGHING IT OUT

In Antarctica, nearly all research is done during the three- to four-month summer season. That's the only time the weather is good enough for supply planes to land. Anyone who doesn't leave on the last plane out in the fall is stuck until the following summer, with no hope of rescue. This means that winter residents endure stormy, freezing, pitch-dark conditions for a solid eight to nine months. Sounds miserable — but don't knock it until you've tried it. "It's a simple lifestyle," says one scientist who likes the winter watch.

RECORD 17

Lowest Temperature on Earth

Located near Earth's magnetic south pole, the Russian-owned ...tok Station in Antarctica is one of the most isolated places in ...world. During the winter, it's also the coldest. Temperatures ...this forsaken spot regularly dip below - 90 degrees ...renheit, and even colder spells have been known to ...he station. Conditions were especially extreme on July ...1983, when Vostok scientists recorded a temperature ...128.6 degrees Fahrenheit, the **Lowest Temperature** ...**Earth**. That's cold enough to freeze human flesh on ...tact! Luckily, the Vostok scientists had enough sense to ...inside and keep their tootsies toasty.

SOUTH AMERICA

AFRICA

ANTARCTICA

AUSTRALIA

Because of the soil similarities between Mars and the Atacama Desert, NASA uses this Earth-based desert as a test site for future missions to the red planet.

This is not a fun run.

Each July, about 100 hardy souls compete in the Atacama Crossing, a seven-day foot race across the arid Atacama Desert in Chile. The course stretches 150 miles through some of the desert's most extreme areas. Race organizers supply water and community tents, but runners must carry their own food, gear, and clothing. It's a grueling event and an expensive one — the entrance fee alone is $2,600 — but plenty of racers still want to give it a try. "It's a test of mental toughness," explained one 2004 participant.

RECORD 18
Driest Place

All deserts are dry places, but Chile's Atacama Desert is the most parched. The **Driest Place** is this strip of parched land, about 100 miles wide and 600 miles long, connecting the Andes Mountains and the Pacific coast. How dry is it? Between 1964 and 2001, the average annual rainfall for the meteorological station in Quillagua, an Atacama outpost, was just 0.02 inch. In 2003, researchers ran the same tests on the Atacama's soil that space probes use on distant planets. They concluded that the soil was completely dead.

DRY COUNTY

The Indian town of Cherrapunji, located a few miles from Mawsynram, is nearly as wet as its record-breaking neighbor during monsoon season. But when the clouds clear each year, the city plunges into a severe water shortage. The dry conditions are caused by deforestation, which is the removal of the area's trees and underbrush. Rain rushes through Cherrapunji without being absorbed and ends up in the downhill nation of Bangladesh. Meanwhile, local residents must either walk miles to find springs or buy bottled water from shops.

RECORD 19

Greatest Annual Rainfall

"Rain, rain, go away!" This children's song might as well be the official anthem of Mawsynram, a town in the northeastern Indian state of Meghalaya. Over the past few years, the hidden city has logged an annual average of 467.4 inches of rain. That's the **Greatest Annual Rainfall** of any place in the world. It's not much fun to live in Mawsynram during the four-month rainy season, when clothes always feel damp, waterlogged matches won't strike, and shoes squish at every step. But conditions are dry and pleasant for the rest of the year, so residents tolerate the temporary torrents.

FACT:

Do you know why rain has an odor? Plant oils escape from rocks and soil during rainfall. We say these oils smell like rain because we notice the scent only in damp conditions.

Some people call it liquid sunshine. Others call it rain.

On September 25, 1997, Arizona's sunshine town of Yuma got a break from its near-constant clear skies when tropical storm Nora rolled through town. This incredibly rare weather event dumped several inches of rainfall across the region. That may not sound like a lot, but it's a flood for Yuma, which usually gets only about 3 to 4 inches of rain per year. The downpour wiped away many of the area's crops and caused about $200 million in damage.

Too much sunlight can cau eye damage. For reason, people w live in sunny area should always wea sunglasses.

RECORD 20
Most Sunshine

If you're thinking about moving to Yuma, Arizona, yo better stock up on suntan lotion. Located in Amer Southwest, this city receives an annual average of 4,055 of a possible 4,456 hours of sunshine per year. Translat Outside of nighttime hours, Yuma is sunny 91 percent of time. That's the **Most Sunshine** of any place in the wo With all this sunny weather, it's not surprising that Yuma hot spot during the summer months. The average daily hig July is 107 degrees under Yuma's cloudless skies — and that the *shade*!

UP CLOSE

We're entering the danger zone with the most extreme weather-
~~re~~ted entries in the Guinness World Records archives. Hit the road with
~~the~~ men and women who chase storms, get caught up in history's most
~~dam~~aging hurricane, and see how bad events can get worse when Earth's
~~we~~ather *really* goes haywire. You'll come away with a whole new appreciation
~~for~~ our planet's power . . . and for the people and creatures surviving it.

RECORD 21
Longest Experience as a Storm Chaser

**30 years...
263 tornadoes...
and counting.**

Veteran storm chaser Gene Moore of San Antonio, Texas, has been following bad weather for more than 30 years. During that period he has seen at least 263 tornadoes, a feat that earned him the Guinness World Record for Most Tornadoes Sighted by One Person. Gene specializes in storm photography and has had pictures published in *Time, National Geographic, Nature,* and many other magazines. He is active during the three months of the year when severe weather is likely to occur. Sometimes Gene goes out alone on his twister-tailing missions, but usually he takes a few friends along. "It's more fun to share the experience with others," he explains.

Tornado warning! To most people, these words me "Run away" or "Seek shelter." But to the men and won known as storm chasers, they mean: "Come and get it!" Sto chasers follow tornadoes and other severe weather systems take pictures and gather scientific data. Most people wo consider this a dangerous job — but to David Hoadley of F Church, Virginia, it's more like a relaxing pastime. David has be chasing storms since 1956, giving him the **Longest Experier as a Storm Chaser** of anyone in the world. This veteran cha holds down a full-time job as a government budget analyst, he takes a few weeks off every spring to look for twisters. Th a hair-raising holiday!

In 1977, David Hoadley founded *Stormtrack* magazine to share his experiences and to explore the topic of storm chasing. As the first forum for chasers, this magazine helped to shape storm chasing into the respected pursuit it is today.

YAHOOS BOO-BOOS

The 1996 movie *Twister* showed daring storm chasers in action. Raking in nearly $500 million worldwide, the thriller was a box-office smash — and extremely unpopular in the storm chaser community. Actual chasers felt that the movie's main characters were reckless, careless, and unprofessional. In the real world, chasers who behave like the ones in *Twister* are nicknamed "yahoos" because they foolishly disregard safety precautions and ignore the unofficial rules of the trade, leading to potential mishaps.

UP CLOSE

UP CLOSE

Times are hard in The Big Easy.

Most of the great Louisiana city of New Orleans was built below sea level. Dams called levees kept nearby Lake Pontchartrain from flooding the city. But when Hurricane Katrina rolled through town on August 29, 2005, some of the levees failed. Water poured into New Orleans, eventually flooding and damaging about 80 percent of the city. As of mid-2006, many city services had not returned to normal in the hardest-hit areas, and one part of town remained closed to its former residents.

Worst Damage Toll om a Cyclone Disaster

en Hurricane Katrina crossed the state of Florida on 29, 2005, it was a Category 1 weakling. After reaching thwater-warm Gulf of Mexico, however, the hurricane blew up into a Category 5 monster — at the time, the strongest Atlantic hurricane ever recorded. The storm had ed by the time it hit the Louisiana coast on August 29, was still strong enough to cause flooding and property tion across Louisiana and Mississippi. According to rs Swiss Re, Katrina's final insurance bill is expected to 45 billion — the **Worst Damage Toll from a Cyclone** er. This figure blows away the previous Guinness Record of $15.5 billion, set after Hurricane devastated southern Florida in 1992.

The ocean surface must be at least 80 degrees Fahrenheit before a hurricane can form.

SCALE STRENGTH

Tropical cyclones are ranked on the Saffir-Simpson Hurricane Scale. Each storm is placed in a category between 1 and 5, with 1 being the weakest and 5 being the strongest. A cyclone fluctuates between stronger and weaker during its lifetime. For this reason, a storm may switch categories many times before it blows itself out. Here's how the numbers of a storm's category and wind speed match up.

ACT:

ical cyclones that form
h of the equator spin in a
nterclockwise direction.
se that form south of the
ator spin clockwise.

CATEGORY		WIND SPEED
1	74–95 mph	
2	96–110 mph	
3	111–130 mph	
4	131–155 mph	
5	156 mph or greater	

UP CLOSE

The 1815 Mount Tambor explosion create caldera, a volcar crater, about 4 m wide and half a mile deep.

Nature can transform a mountain into a lethal weapon.

Indonesia has more active volcanoes than any other nation. Mount Tambora is located on the island of Sumbawa, and its volcanic eruption in 1815 vaporized a large part of the mountain, with the aftereffects severely altering the world's weather. Before the blast, the peak of Mount Tambora stretched about 13,000 feet into the sky. After the eruption, the volcano was missing nearly 9,000 feet. Do the math and you'll see that more than a mile of mountaintop disappeared in one extreme instant. This event brings a whole new meaning to the phrase "blown away!"

RECORD 23

Greatest Recorded Climatic Impact of a Volcanic Eruption

A sunny day became a fiery, choking night when Mount Tam erupted on April 10, 1815. The brutal blast instantly destr several cities, killed 10,000 people, and wiped out all plan on neighboring islands — and that was just a warm-up. Ove next few months, ashes from the eruption spread throug Earth's atmosphere, blocking the sun's rays and dropping g average temperatures as much as 5.4 degrees Fahrenheit. The 1816 came to be known as "the year without a summer" v cold conditions led to crop failure — and then to starvatio throughout Europe and North America. By the time the Grea **Recorded Climatic Impact of a Volcanic Eruption** subs an estimated 92,000 people had died, making this event on the greatest natural disasters in recorded history.

BIG BANG

The Mount Tambora eruption was a hiccup compared to a world-changing volcanic belch that took place 75,000 years ago. A supervolcano on the Indonesian island of Sumatra blew its top, filling the skies with more than 670 cubic miles of matter — about 28 times the amount released by Mount Tambora. There is evidence that this event caused a mini ice age that almost wiped out the human race.

FACT:

Magma is molten rock still contained inside Earth's layers that has not yet erupted from a volcano. Once the molten rock reaches open air, it becomes lava.

Life, and the Heat Index, has its ups and downs.

Earth's average temperature changes over time. When temperatures are high, the planet's surface is fairly ice-free. When temperatures drop, ice sheets called glaciers spread out from the north and south poles. The lower the average temperature, the farther the glaciers spread. Glacier periods are called ice ages, and Earth is in the middle of one now. Luckily for us, the planet is currently enjoying a warm patch — but don't expect it to last forever. Scientists say it could get mighty chilly in another 10,000 years or so.

RECORD 24
Longest Ice Age

Planet Earth may have been Snowball Earth 2.3 or 2 billion years ago. Evidence suggests that a severe ice age hit t globe around this time, blanketing the continents with glaci and freezing the upper 2,500 feet of every ocean. From spac the planet would have looked like a white ball instead of t blue-green orb we see today. The frigid phase lasted abo 70 million years — the **Longest Ice Age** in Earth's histo Scientists believe that one-celled plants started the snowy sp by releasing oxygen. This gas changed the atmosphere and a lo of trapped warmth escaped. It's the global equivalent of your parent telling you, "Hey, close the door! You're letting the heat out." Now you know what can happen if you — and the world — forget to close that door.

The USA's Great Lakes were originally glaciers.

SURF'S UP

Glaciers that cover large land masses are called **continental ice sheets.** Today, there are just two continental ice sheets, one in Greenland and one in Antarctica. The expansive Greenland sheet would raise sea levels nearly 20 feet if it melted. But that's just a drop in the bucket compared to the Antarctic ice sheet, which would raise sea levels an incredible 213 feet if it melted!

Warm periods between major ice ages can be millions of years long.

FACT:

A chilly period named the Little Ice Age started around the year 1300 and lasted until 1850. During this cold stretch, major rivers around the world often froze solid during the wintertime.

Pick a theory, any theory.

Explanations for the Permian-Triassic extinction event include:

- A giant meteor or comet that struck the Antarctic.
- An exploding star that flooded Earth with deadly radiation.
- An intense volcanic period that changed Earth's climate.
- The release of lethal gases from the ocean floor.

Some scientists even think the correct answer might be "all of the above." They believe that a bunch of disasters struck Earth around the same time. Let's hope they're right. The wilder the coincidence, the less likely it is to happen again.

The Permian Triassic extinct event is someti called the Great Dying.

RECORD 25
Greatest Mass Extinction

About 248 million years ago, at the end of the Permian geolog period, living conditions on our planet changed dramatically. results were devastating. Animals everywhere began dying, within a million years, at least 90 percent of the planet's o species and 70 percent of its higher land animals had disappea This episode is known as the Permian-Triassic extinction event, it was the **Greatest Mass Extinction** ever to occur. It is also of science's biggest mysteries. Many researchers have searched answers, but no one has come up with a perfect explanatio what happened eons ago. Unless someone invents a time mach this is one puzzle that may remain unsolved.

ZOOM OUT!

Although our book ends here, your exploration of the wildest record-breakers in rain, wind, cold, and heat can continue among the online archives (www.guinnessworldrecords.com) and within the pages of *Guinness World Records*.

Go up close and get involved — it's your world!

Photo Credits

The publisher would like to thank the following for their
kind permission to use their photographs in this book:

Cover, title page (main), 7 (top panel background) Lightning Cityscape © Punchstock, (inset)
Lightning Bolt © Mike Theiss/Jim Reed Photography/CORBIS; 3 Bird Under Umbrella © Cynthia
Diane Pringle/CORBIS; 4 Grouse © Peggi Miller/iStockphoto; 5 (middle) Rainstorm Survivors
© Koji Sasahara/AP Photo, (right) Lightning Strike © Steve Bloom/Taxi/Getty Images, (left),
10 Snowstorm © Michael S. Yamashita/CORBIS; 5 – 11 Storm Cloud Background, 29 (left)
Clouded Sun, 29 – 34 Raindrop Background, 35 – 44 Glacier Background © Morguefile.com;
6 Fossilized Raindrops Courtesy of John and Henry from J&H PaleoScience/digsfossils.com; 7
(bottom) Boy Catching Raindrops © Ellen Denuto/Iconica/Getty Images; 8 Illustration © Chase
Studio/Photo Researchers, Inc., Fulgurite © Wikipedia/Creative Commons; 9 Hailstone, 35
(left), 36 Storm Chasers © Jim Reed/CORBIS; 10 Snowflake © Royalty-Free/CORBIS; 12 (left)
Waterspout © Dr. Joseph Golden/NOAA, (middle) Tornado © A.T. Willett/Image Bank/Getty
Images, (right) Honduras Hurricane © Victor R. Caivano/AP Photo; 13 Mount Washington
© Christopher J. Morris/CORBIS; 14 Waterspout © Mohammed Zaatari/AP Photo, Illustration
© Mary Evans/Photo Researchers, Inc.; 15 Tornado © Warren Faidley/Oxford Scientific Films,
Super Outbreak Survivor © Bettmann/CORBIS; 16 Tornado © A.T. Willett/Alamy; 18, 19 (bottom)
Neptune, 20 (right), 26, 27 Jupiter's Great Red Spot, 21 Boomerang Nebula © JPL/NASA; 19
(top) God Neptune © National Geographic/Getty Images; 20 (left) Comet Hale Bopp © Dan
Schechter/Photo Researchers, Inc., (main) Aurora Borealis © Jack Finch/Photo Researchers, Inc.;
20 – 28 Space Background, 24 (bottom) Geomagnetic Storm Illustration © NASA; 21 Boomerang
Nebulae Up Close © NASA, ESA, and The Hubble Heritage Team; 22 Sun's Internal Core
Illustration © M. Kulyk/Photo Researchers, Inc.; 23 The Planets © George Toubalis/iStockphoto;
24 (top) Geomagnetic Sun Storm © NASA/AP Photo; 28 Venus © Digital Vision/Picture Quest;
29 (middle) Chuquicamata, Chile © Charles O'Rear/CORBIS, (right) Penguins © Australian
Antarctic Division/AP Photo; 30 Sahara Desert © Martin Harvey/CORBIS; 31 Vostok Weather
Station © Josh Landis, National Science Foundation, Mount Vinson © Gordon Wiltsie/National
Geographic Image Collection; 32 Atacama Desert, Chile © Bruce Coleman, USA; 33 Rainstorm
Playtime © Fat Chance Productions/Iconica/Getty Images; 34 Desert Solar Eclipse © Richard
Cummins/CORBIS, Kids in Shades © Maureen Lawrence/Jupiter Images; 35 (middle) Woolly
Mammoth Tusks Excavated © Francis Latreille/Novi Productions/REUTERS, (right) Kilauea
Volcano © Soames Summerhays/Photo Researchers, Inc.; 37 (top) David Hoadley Courtesy of
David Hoadley, (bottom) Twister © WB/UNIVERSAL/AMBLIN/THE KOBAL COLLECTION; 38
(top) Volunteer Rescuer in New Orleans © Eric Gay/AP Photo, (bottom right) Devastated New
Orleans Neighborhood © Rob Carr/AP Photo, (bottom left) Flooded City Aerial View © Gary
Nichols, U.S. Navy/AP Photo; 39 Hurricane Katrina © NOAA; 40 Tambora island © CNES 2002;
41 Lava Fountain © Krafft/Photo Researchers, Inc.; 42 Woolly Mammoth Replica © Jonathan
Blair/CORBIS; 44 Asteroid Impacts Earth Illustration © David A. Hardy, Futures: 50 Years in Space/
Photo Researchers, Inc.; 45 Girl Under Umbrella © Colin Hawkins/Taxi/Getty Images.

Be a Record-Breaker!

Message from the Keeper of the Records:

cord-breakers are the ultimate in one way or another — the youngest, the oldest, the
lest, the smallest. So how do you get to be a record-breaker? Follow these important steps:

1. Before you attempt your record, check with us to make sure your record is suitable and
e. Get your parents' permission. Next, contact one of our officials by using the record
plication form at www.guinnessworldrecords.com.

2. Tell us about your idea. Give us as much information as you can, including what the record
when you want to attempt it, where you'll be doing it, and other relevant information.
   a) We will tell you if a record already exists, what safety guidelines you must follow during
   your attempt to break that record, and what evidence we need as proof that you
   completed your attempt.
   b) If your idea is a brand-new record nobody has set yet, we need to make sure it meets
   our requirements. If it does, then we'll write official rules and safety guidelines specific
   to that record idea and make sure all attempts are made in the same way.

3. Whether it is a new or existing record, we will send you the guidelines for your selected
cord. Once you receive these, you can make your attempt at any time. You do not need a
inness World Record official at your attempt. But you do need to gather evidence. Find out
re about the kind of evidence we need to see by visiting our website.

4. Think you've already set or broken a record? Put all of your evidence as specified by the
idelines in an envelope and mail it to us at Guinness World Records.

5. Our officials will investigate your claim fully — a process that can take up to a few weeks,
pending on the number of claims we've received, and how complex your record is.

6. If you're successful, you will receive an official certificate that says you are now a Guinness
orld Record-holder!

Need more info? Check out www.guinnessworldrecords.com for lots more hints, tips, and some
p record ideas. Good luck!